Energy Every Day

Table of Contents

by Emma Rose

Getting Started

Imagine that you and your family are at an amusement park. You are standing in line. You are waiting for your turn on your favorite ride—the roller coaster!

Soon the roller coaster glides to a stop, and you get into your seat. Safety bars slide down to hold you in place. The roller coaster begins to move. You grip the safety bars tightly.

A chain pulls the roller coaster up, up, up the track. At the top, the roller coaster stops for just a second. Then it hurtles down one slope and up the next. One thing powers both you and the roller coaster—**energy**.

Energy and You

In science, energy means that someone or something is doing work. Everything you do—running, playing ball, and even sleeping—takes energy.

You get your energy from the food you eat. Food is the fuel your body burns to get the **chemical energy** you need. You need that chemical energy to live, grow, work, and have fun.

Plants get energy from the sun. Some plants are foods we eat. When we eat vegetables, salad greens, or even popcorn, energy from those plants goes into our bodies.

Some animals eat plants, too. When they do, they get energy from the plants. Then if we eat meat or dairy products from these animals, that energy is passed on to us.

Using and Saving Energy

Look up. Are the lights on? If so, that's **electricity** at work! Electricity is a form of energy. Electricity powers things like lamps, fans, computers, water heaters, and furnaces. It may even power some of your toys!

Every day we need to use a lot of electricity. So it's important not to waste it. Why? Because natural resources like oil and coal are used to make electricity. And we need to conserve, or save, our natural resources. We can do this by saving energy, not wasting it.

A recycling center

School Recycling Program

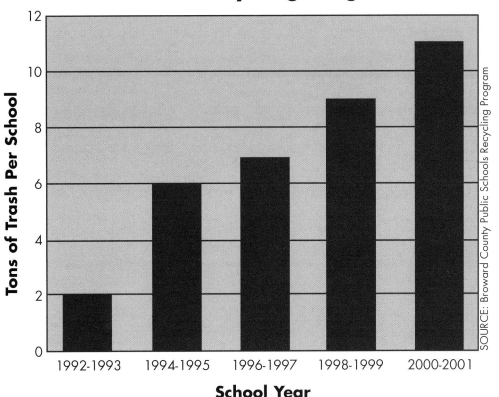

SOURCE: Broward County Public Schools Recycling Program

Perhaps you turn off lights to save energy. Many people recycle things to save energy, too. Look at this graph. It shows how much trash some schools collected for recycling.

Energy at Play

Do you and your friends play soccer? It takes a lot of energy to play soccer. It also takes many kinds of energy. As you run down the field, you use **kinetic energy**—the energy of motion.

You use chemical energy, too. The chemical energy in your body gives you muscle power!

You also use **mechanical energy**. Your muscles use this kind of energy when they work. For example, mechanical energy lifts your feet and pumps your arms.

Even though this soccer ball is not moving, it has **potential energy**, or the *possibility* to do work. One way an object gets potential energy is when you raise it above the ground. It has the potential of falling to the ground.

Potential energy is also the energy that is stored in an object. One way to store energy is in a battery. By itself, a battery has potential energy.

Think about putting a battery in a toy, such as a remote-control car. The car now has potential energy. Turn the battery on and press the button on the control. Electricity from the battery makes the car move. The energy stored in the battery changed the car's potential energy to kinetic energy—the energy of motion.

Energy All Around

Stand in the sun for a while. The sun's heat warms you and the earth. The sunlight helps you see in the daytime. We call energy from the sun **solar energy**.

It's important for scientists to find many ways to use solar energy. Solar energy may be used instead of oil or other fuels that come from our natural resources. And since solar energy comes from the sun, we will always have plenty of it to use.

How do you use energy? Perhaps you enjoy playing with remote-control cars. Or are you a batter swinging at a baseball? No matter what you do, energy makes it happen.

Index